Coastal Bend Winter Haiku

poems & photographs

Judith Lauter

to Ken

my dear travel companion on every flyway

To order additional copies of this book, contact:
Xlibris LLC
1-888-795-4274
www.Xlibris.com
Orders@Xlibris.com

Contents

Preface

More species of birds make their winter home in Texas than in any other state. Nueces County, located on the Texas Coastal Bend, receives so many species from the Missouri/Mississippi and the Central Flyways of North America that for the last 10 years the National Audubon Society has declared it and the county seat Corpus Christi the "birdiest" county and city in the nation.

Padre Island, the barrier island that lies just off the Gulf coast at this point, extends approximately 113 miles south. It is not only the longest barrier island in the world, but the Padre Island National Seashore, which protects the majority of the island, makes it the longest *undeveloped* barrier island. Many migrating birds overwinter on Padre Island and adjacent areas, while still others use this coastline as a dependable stopover on flights destined for even further south. In all, Padre Island provides a seasonal home to more than 380 bird species – about half of all those found in the United States. In addition, migrating insects such as the monarch butterfly also depend on the plains, beaches, and wetlands of the Coastal Bend for support during their long travels.

While I was growing up in Austin TX, my family made its own migrations to the Coastal Bend. My dad was a hobby fisherman, so we regularly visited Gulf beaches around Corpus Christi – and one of my earliest memories is my mom and grandmother laying out a picnic lunch on a warm beach, while my dad waded into the surf to try his luck.

After my parents moved us to Michigan, I did not live in Texas again for almost 50 years, but all that time the Gulf Coast remained alive in my memory as a beautiful, somewhat vague image of blue sky, green sea, and long, curving beaches – much the way it may appear in the minds of the many birds who return here year after year, to make their winter home.

So when Ken and I moved back to Texas in 2001, one of the first things I wanted to do was take our own flyway to Corpus – and we have been spending a month or so around Christmas here ever since. It has been a vivifying seasonal migration for us, and we learn more about the coast and its amazing diversity of weathers, plants, and animals, every time we come.

— *JLL, Corpus Christi TX, December 2013*

Coastal Bend Winter Haiku

Morning

Morning Siren Call

Out of the mist, tempting sounds:
rain, gull cries, waves that
ask how far we want to go.

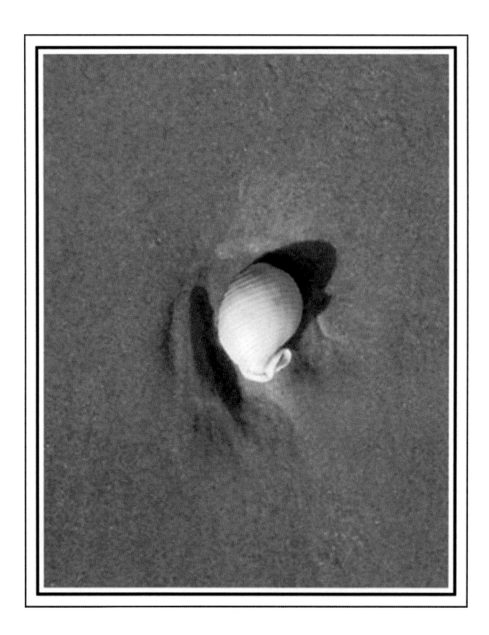

Shell

Someone's house left to wind and
tide: tragedy, or
just a change of domicile?

Mathematics in Motion

Like the ocean, pelicans-
in-line find waves are
best for moving place to place.

Water Birds

Clearwater wavelets like a
wing extended, sand's
own gold feathers underneath.

Sanderling on the Go

Flown down from High Arctic, vast
continent passing
below, to trot this warm sand.

Sandpipers Don't Surf

When lion manes of waves get
too close, pipers show
zebra wings – and fly away.

Dance in Air

In a brisk wind, herring gull
rises, brakes, and turns,
matching water wing for wing.

Midday

The Original

White gull waves away grey clouds,
knows gullwing design
shows best when drawn against blue.

View from the Dunes

Out there the wide blue sea; up
here, land these plants hold
tight, it seems so easy lost.

Out of the Wind

Best place on bright, cool days – skin
on warm sand, sunning
your soft shell, like a turtle.

Tracks in Sand

Someone else has been walking
here, relaxing: wing-
tips dragging, barefoot, like me.

Checkered-White Butterfly

Chooses dunes for snacks and sun:
wingback reflectors
keep her warm enough to fly.

Beach Evening Primrose

Yellow blooms must be their own
butterflies: monarchs
long since flown to Michoacán.

Afternoon

Texas Palmetto at the Birding Center

Old brown wings folded down, new
green ones spread, catching
sugar from sweet winter sun.

Blue-Winged Teal's Time-Out

Through calm light, returns to nest
in the reeds, warm fresh-
water wings ripple him home.

Heron and Sandpiper

Stand still together – only
small ripples disturb
their reflections on winter.

White and Pink

Spoonbills start out snowy white
as egrets, but soon
their pink-shelled food dyes them rose.

Evening

Safe Harbor

Body-warm satin water
holds sun's heat all night
long, though dark falls soft as snow.

Evening Pelican

In late light pelican banks
overhead, floating
on blue tides of rising air.

Nautilus Sunset

Sky like a shell – dark blue, pink,
green, lips touching cool
seawater, curling toward night.

Moon's Migration

Our last night – white egret moon
rises on her own
flyway, always facing home.

Epilogue

56

Flyways and Watersheds

1. Flyways

The waters warm, the waters
cool, and flows begin – currents
of sea, air, animals. In the north, birds

sometimes in ones, sometimes
in Vs, or flocks like clouds –
take wing, rising in widening

circles, scanning for magnetic lines
or slants of light to point out the flyway
where the warm that went first has

already flown south. And so they fly,
the furthest north starting over arctic taiga,
its scattered spruce sticking up

from mile after mile of wetlands, sun
winking in ponds, marshes, creeks
passing underneath, then further south, dark forests,

then grasslands mile after mile, always
ponds and rivers for landmarks,
stopovers to rest and eat on the way ever south.

Then finally a brilliant horizon all light, the sea
seen from afar, then the coast appears,
a curve of brown against blue with a fine

white line between, beaches, and bordering
wetlands, ponds with warm water.
Some set down briefly then leave to go

further south, compasses in their heads
calling them on. But others settle in here
for the winter, a second home known and trusted – food

and good water and warmth – warmth: even on grey
rainy cold days, nothing like what it is
now in the north they left.

All winter they float and feed,
living their lives, supported, sustained.
Then one day in spring when lengthening days

send the signals for returning, they rise, they
climb up again the stairs of the air, and fly
back thousands of miles north,

to the other known places – food
and good water and warmth – living
their lives, supported and sustained.

2. Watersheds

Snow, ice, falls and melts, rain
falls, and flows begin. In the far north
trickles become creeks then rivers, flowing

along lines drawn by rocks, watersheds,
wrinkles in the land risen above the sea
that guide land's water back to its original home,

the sea surrounding all. The rivers of central
Canada's MacKenzie Plain flow opposite winter flight paths,
north toward the Arctic –

but south of the Eastern Divide (from western
Montana to Lake Superior) waters flow east, toward
the Missouri and big brown Mississippi, in their rush to the Gulf.

South of that, below the Red River spanning
Texas east to west, the rivers point southeast, draining
the basin of seas from 60 million years ago,

and all along the warm curve of the "third coast"
release their fresh silver into the Gulf's salty green.
But then as the sun moves and the earth turns, waters

return, like cranes, like egrets – in cool
and warm they rise, from the waves
of the Gulf, from coastal wetlands, marshes, rivers,

sometimes invisible, sometimes in clouds like flocks,
streaming, circling, climbing into layers
that cruise with the jet stream, currents

that move as the earth moves, flows and eddies
forming, un-forming, constantly moving, the ocean of air.
Witness this great migration – step outside: <u>see</u> flocks

of rain-grey clouds flying overhead; <u>feel</u> rain feathering
your face; <u>hear</u> the sigh and hiss of air
passing overhead – the sound of wings.

Notes

Shell p. 9 – Scotch Bonnet (*Semicassis granulata granulata*), a marine snail of the subfamily *Cassinae*

Mathematics in Motion p. 11 – Brown Pelican (*Pelecanus occidentalis*)

Sanderling on the Go p. 15 – Sanderling (*Calidris alba*), circumpolar breeder; migrates to South America, Southern Europe, Africa, Australia

Sandpipers Don't Surf p. 17 – Willet Sandpiper (*Tringa semipalmata*); these light brown birds [cf. top of photo p. 40] do not reveal their wings' dramatic striping until they fly

Dance in Air p. 19 – American Herring Gull (*Larus argentatus smithsonianus*)

The Original p. 23 – Ring-Billed Gull (*Larus delawarensis*)

View from the Dunes p. 25 – foreground plant is Sea Purslane (*Sesuvium portulacastrum*), a perennial herb with antibacterial and antifungal properties, which is pickled and eaten in the Philippines as *atchara*

Checkered-White Butterfly p. 31 – (*Pontia protodice*), uses "reflectance basking" in which sunlight—reflecting wings are held at a certain angle to direct sunlight onto the body, to achieve the 30-40 degrees C needed for flight – *Wikipedia. 2013;* the plant is Sea Rocket (*Cakile edentula*), a member of the mustard family, nutritious for humans as well as *Pontia*

Beach Evening Primrose p. 33 – (*Oenothera drummondi*), named for Thomas Drummond (1790—1835), an early Texas naturalist; monarch butterflies (*Danaus plexippus*) may migrate more than 3,000 miles (3-4 generations) – those from the central U.S. and southern Canada gather into a central flyway over Texas, and winter in the Sierra Madre mountains of the southwestern Mexican states of Mexico and Michoacán (migration research by F. & N. Urquhart, K.C. Brugger, C. Trail – cf. *Wikipedia article on monarchs, 2013*)

Texas Palmetto at the Birding Center p. 37– (*Sabal mexicana*), featured in the Audubon Sabal Palm Sanctuary in Brownsville TX

Blue-Winged Teal's Time-Out p. 39 – (*Anas discors*), likes to winter on freshwater marshes with bulrushes and cattails for cover

Heron and Sandpiper p. 41 – Tricolored Heron (*Egretta tricolor*) and Willet Sandpiper (*Tringa semipalmata)*

White and Pink p. 43 – Snowy Egrets (*Egretta thula*) and Roseate Spoonbills (*Platalea ajaja*); like flamingos, spoonbills eat brine shrimp that in turn eat algae containing the carotenoid pigments astaxanthin and canthaxanthin, accounting for the birds' color

Evening Pelican p. 49 – White Pelican (*Pelecanus erythrorhynchos*)

Printed in the United States
By Bookmasters